Ing is still King

ing

is still king

Word Play

By: AJ Crigler

Ing is still King

By: A J Crigler

Ing is still King

Artwork and story by: A J Crigler
StoryTime Publications
P.O. Box 1644
Miamisburg, OH 45343-1644

ISBN-13: 978-0615985367
ISBN-10: 061598536X

This book was printed in the United States of America.

To order additional copies of this book, contact: AJ Crigler at

email: ajcstorytimepublications@aol.com

Ing is still King
By: A J Crigler

Long ago in days of yore

there lived a prince named Ing;

instead of speaking like most people did

he loved to sing everything.

Good morning world, what a glorious day.
I slept all night, now I'm on my way.

He greeted his mother with a kiss each day

and then he began to sing,

"It's a glorious morn." he would ring out

as he annoyed his father the king.

It's a glorious morn

"Why do you have to sing all the time,"

asked his father, the king?

"Why can't you be like everyone else

and speak those thoughts you bring."

"I cannot help it father,

because this is my thing,

for you named me Ing

and it rhymes with sing."

Ing left the castle

to go mingle with the others.

He'd fling a ball around

and then linger with his brothers.

Ing loved to hear

the church bells ring;

and with each ping he'd sing

ring-a-ding-ding.

ring-a-ding-ding

ring-a-ding-ding

ring-a-ding-ding

The king was very worried

for the young prince, Ing.

Would the people mock him

because he loved to sing?

One day Ing and his brothers

went riding to a spring fling.

They ran into a big hive

and Ing got a painful bee sting.

His neck began to swell

like a big ripe melon

and he nearly fell off his horse

as he ran for his life like a felon.

All the kingdom was saddened,

because the prince could not sing.

The people started singing their words,

to bring a smile to their prince, Ing.

Good morning Prince Ing

We're sorry you can't sing

We hope you'll feel better

from your bee sting.

23

The king saw how much the people cared

and allowed them all to sing.

So he was no longer annoyed,

and honored his son, the next king.

Goodnight Kingdom, Goodnight!

Of thee I sing

Goodnight to all the world

for I am your King, Ing

26

The End

Ing is still King

Ing is still King (IISK) is a word play story about a prince who loved to rhyme and sing. It was something that made him happy, but it annoyed his father the king. The word play for the day is words that end in I-N-G. It is a learning experience for children 6-12 and also some adults.

In writing *(IISK)* it took about 4 hours to write the poem/story, but the pictures are always more of a challenge and takes a lot of time. Writing and illustrating is something that makes me happy. It is exciting to develop pictures to go with the poems and a joy to see the story come together. It is a fictional fantasy and I hope everyone will enjoy ***Ing is still King*** as much as I did creating it.

Reading is essential to life.

Story Time **Publications**